CL

Understanding the student and making a breakthrough

SBPC

Simms Books Publishing Corporation

SBPC

SIMMS BOOKS PUBLISHING CORP.

Publishers Since 2012

Published By Simms Books Publishing

Jonesboro, GA

Copyright ©James R Simms, 2023

2023951485

Library of Congress Cataloging in Publication Data

James R Simms

Class Clowns

Understanding the student and making a breakthrough

ISBN: 978-1-949433-55-5

Printed in the United States of America

Book Arrangement by Simms Books Publishing

Cover by Mikhail Simms

Edited by Janice Green-Davis

Help is on the way...

Table of Contents

Foreword

First, after reading *Class Clowns* I understand the importance of the supporting cast; The introvert (Recluse) is a category all of their own, as is the Copy Cat. I have taught all three types as well as the Bully (Angry Child). Each type of child requires individual learning experiences, as many as you mentioned. The second thing that I would encourage would be the need to have teamwork among the parents, students, and teachers that would begin the first week of school. Everyone should cheer for each other.

Teaching is a collaborative act and the students can achieve if everyone is pulling in the same direction. In many ways, a teacher is like the conductor of an orchestra of "learners". Each child is their own instrument and needs time to shine and be seen and heard.

The Class Clown is a natural leader and finding ways for them to shine is IMPERATIVE not only for their sake but the sake of the success of the class!

--*Mary Myers Wright, Barcroft Elementary 4th Grade Teacher, Class of 85'*

Introduction

Teachers have one of the most challenging careers in the world, being responsible for teaching, molding, and growing young minds. Let's talk about the next challenge; dealing with a Class Clown. Now in this short book, we will give a new face to the Class Clown and how their disruptive behavior has a source and how to tap into the genius and gain some understanding and see eye to eye with your Class Clown. Let us not forget the other children who go unattended.

Recognize the signs

For you to solve a problem you have to have all of the facts, then training and experience. In a perfect world, the training part would be nice but as you all know some situations you will just have to experience and your results come with trial and error. As a teacher, you are a detective, sniffing out the clues to address issues that may arise in the classroom, your assessment of the child's learning abilities, and drawing up a course of action to get them to a desired destination; becoming literate, affluent and knowledgeable in a particular subject matter is your end goal. Along the way you use all the tools you have at hand whether it's adjusted modifications, standard-based grading, and or tiered instruction which works the majority of the time. Then as you all are aware; life throws you a curve ball.

You have that one child and if you are lucky maybe 2 or 3 of them and if you are just on the naughty list, you may have your hands full. This child is very disruptive and in most cases is seen as the Class Clown. We are going to use this name in the context of a disruptive child, the Class Clown.

I've had a belief system instilled in me from my mother that what you do at home is what you will do out in the streets. So, understanding that logic and putting it into practice when you are dealing with a Class Clown is very important. It starts at home. Now I know what you are thinking. You are right! You don't live in that home and cannot change that child's reality and respect for school, his teachers, his or her peers, and anyone else outside of their home. Sounds like a tall order, being successful in turning this child's behavior and outlook around. So here is where your training kicks in.

You have done the work; you have assessed the issue and now you are working on a plan to help this child who is known as the Class Clown. Now in your planning, you have to first lay all the extenuating factors on the table and look at home first. I know your job is to teach and not be a counselor, head doctor, or therapist. Wrong! A great teacher is all of those wrapped up in one and a brilliant troubleshooter, you have to come up with a plan of action.

In this example, you have a child whose behavior in class is so disruptive you are constantly sending them to the office, and now you finally get to speak with the child's parent.

Brace yourself for the encounter, you will find the answers to that child's behavior issues.

The Angry Child

"Somebody called for an exorcist? No, I have run out of holy water this cross does not seem to help at all. What am I to do?"

No one said that I would need to be a practicing MMA fighter, part-time referee, therapist, and priest! Just a few words from overwhelmed teachers who may have Angry Children in their classrooms. What is the solution? These children wake up with violence on their minds and are not afraid to express that violence anytime someone looks their way. To deal with this kid you have to shift the angry energy to something more productive... but how?? Naturally, the Angry Child would love nothing more than to be left alone, from their classmates and you, but don't honor that request. Here is what you do, since they have all of that spunk with them, call a meeting with the parent and principal. Let's get to the bottom of this issue.

"…Brian can you please take your seat. I am trying to instruct the class on how to draw their maps."

"Nobody cares about no maps, forget you and your maps! (Yes, this is the PG version) I ain't got to be quiet I will do what I want!"

Now this has not been your first problem with Brian, and for sure won't be your last. It has gotten to a tipping point and you have noticed that not only has the children in your class suffered from instruction being interrupted more times than you can count during the day, but you see he is ramping it up even more each day—time to call a meeting.

Finally, you can get Brian's mom to meet with you, it has been 5 long weeks since the first request has gone out and she has refused each one. The issue: Brian's mother has her side of the story and from what she has shared with the principal and whomever she can get to listen, that you the teacher are the source of all of his problems and that you are always picking on her son.

Now let's do a checkup from the neck up and question one's self, Am I doing all that I can to reach this child or have I checked out yet? Now go into the meeting with a heart and mind to listen. Be as assertive as you can to let the parent know what your expectations are for their son or daughter. Take a deep breath and go for it!

The proof is in the pudding...

The meeting happens and Brian's mom is on a roll...She spends most of her time regurgitating a one-sided account about all of his run-ins with you the teacher. She banters on, 'This was unfair; he was not able to go on the field trip, spending all day in *I.S.S.,* and him feeling targeted by you the teacher.' Finally, she takes time to catch her breath and wants your time to speak to address all of her unfounded claims of being hard and biased with her son.

Taking in a deep breath, you want to approach this with caution doing your best to not insight another 20 minutes of ranting. Now at this time, you can gather that it will be a one-sided deal with mother and son and everyone else is the blame and never her son. He hasn't been in school long enough to build a mindset that every teacher is after him or doesn't like him, but as you can see whatever he says his mother will finish his fight. Now you have to be very careful with your questioning and or even your side of the story. Let's try this approach, since they are playing by the same playbook, just what if Brian is displaying a fear or experience that his mother had gone through as a child and she is projecting to protect her child and in turn just creating a bigger issue?

P.E.N.S.

Here you will need to use the **P.E.N.S.** method:

Patience- this goes a long way. Keeping yourself from becoming unhinged, know that this will take some time.

Empathy – you will learn what the problem may be and work on understanding the root cause and problem.

New – remember you are not the person who hurt them in the past, you are a new teacher with a fresh start to make it right.

Solution – everyone wants to have it their way, Let give the people what they want while coming up with great ways to deal with their insecurities and make it plain how you want to help and not do harm.

"Ms. Johnson, where are you from, and how was your relationship with your teachers at Brian's age?"

She takes the floor again, speaking about her childhood and she could count on one hand how many good teachers she had growing up, the engagement between teacher and student was horrible. Her instinct to protect her child and project her fears onto her son has caused him to be defensive and a problem child. She reiterates that she has told her son that if anyone touches him to fight them back whether student or teacher. Now we can understand the root cause of why Brain is disrespectful in class and has no respect for others. Without offending Ms. Johnson, what should be your next statement? We have to earn Mom's trust also; she has had a history of trauma connected to her childhood when it came to school and teachers.

"Ms. Johnson, thank you for giving us some much-needed insight, we are here to help and would never treat Brian that way, we understand how you feel and what you went through. We want the best for Brian and can assure you that we will not put him in a bad situation, we are here to listen to him and help him. This is a safe place; Brian is a bright young man who just needs to apply himself and he will do great things in life with all of our support. We believe in Brian and are invested in him to have the best future possible. Now with your help Ms. Johnson we will do our best to make sure Brian becomes the best cancer research doctor ever. Yes, we are paying attention we just need him to know that we are not the bad guys we want and need his help in the classroom, he is a born leader so let us help him lead in the right way. Can we depend on you, Ms. Johnson? You can depend on us to teach your son and support him."

"Well, I don't know what to do, I'm no teacher I barely made it out of high school myself, I don't know what I can do to help him."

"Well, that's the beauty of it all, Ms. Johnson, you only have to do some small things and we know that Brian will be able to pick up on the rest."

"I need you to remember this and we will also send a packet home that will drive home the importance of these three words. Listen, Encourage, and Remind. Brian wants to get what's on his mind out so just listen, then encourage him that he is a great child, wanted and needed, and remind him that these skills when used properly will get him closer each day to his life's goals. You becoming his biggest cheerleader will help him process his anger and perception that the world is not out to get him, well at least not the one at home or here at school. Mama Bear is projecting her experience onto her child making him unruly."

By now she should know that you are not the enemy and Brian is safe in your care, she can forgive herself and take a deep breath, knowing that Brian has great teachers who only want the best for him. Him being challenged is not being picked on you see his potential and want him to grow in his purpose.

There is always a history behind the actions of a child, what's happening at home, and the trauma of their parent being passed down to them as a defense mechanism. When you uncover the issues, you will have a better understanding and know where you can be an ally and not an enemy.

The Recluse

The Class Clown is not always the center of attention, he or she may be the quiet child. The Recluse sits back and watches what's going on in the classroom, sometimes they are withdrawn from classroom activities, it's a mixed bag, because he or she still keeps up with homework and aces the test, or it can be the child on the other end of the spectrum that fails every task. I always believe that there is always something else; conditions at home, low self-esteem, a multiple of other problems in his or her life that influence their behavior The hard job is to get the Recluse both out of their comfort zone and finding what makes them tic. Now I know, you have over 20 children in your classroom and it is almost impossible to concentrate on just one. Well, this will take some time and great classroom management on your part even some background detective work, talking to their parents, counselor, and even his or her teachers from the year before to see if there was a change from one year to the next.

Believe it or not, you will have to deal with the Recluse with great compromise, yes you might have to do what the child is interested in, don't worry there is a formula to this, patience plus interest equals a trustworthy outcome. The number one roadblock for most Recluse is that they have no shoulder to cry on or even an ear to listen to them. It will take time to help them open up, show your interest in them, wanting and needing to know what's going on while guaranteeing them that you care will earn that trust. To keep this newfound relationship going, you have to give the Recluse a job. Yes, keep them busy and they will start to open up. Have them help with passing out papers and collecting them. Work on The Recluse can be themselves or the best version of themselves when they are comfortable and know that someone cares.

It is imperative as a teacher that you learn the skillset of being a counselor and therapist. I know you signed up to just teach, sorry to bust your bubble, it will take more than that and some say it's gonna take a miracle.

Unfortunately, we all live in the real world, and in most cases, there are certain sections of the population you serve who live in complete turmoil. There are plenty of factors that are the causes, but you now have to deal with the effects and fallout.

As a parent, this harsh reality is one that I cringe about whenever the thought comes to mind of SA and MA, (sexual abuse and mental abuse). I cringe and feel a burning sensation in the pit of my stomach, then I feel sick. How could this happen to such a small being who hasn't figured out who they can trust? So, keep in mind that your Recluse may be a victim and they are not intentionally unattached it's their defense mechanism.

Your training day begins…

The school year has started without any unnecessary drama, it has been a week now and you can audit your classroom, from their likes, dislikes, personalities, and forecasts of each individual work ethic, you know this class. Mrs. Turnip has given you a full report from last year's roster, you know the attentive students, the ones who get good grades and the ones who at least try, this year you have a lively bunch. You have two new students, take time to figure them out. This is one of the most challenging relationships that you will have to build on trust and be a safe refuge for the student.

"Ok class I need you all to turn to page 10 of your book, and I need you to answer the questions at the end of the chapter."

You notice that your student has not opened up their book, and after a few minutes goes by the class is busy at work as the student looks down at her desk. Now would be a good time to call the student to the side and inquire not make a scene or reprimand. Upon your questioning you see that she is very timid and withdrawn, she doesn't open completely up at this time but over the next few weeks, stay consistent and she will. Earning her trust and getting her to believe that your classroom is a safe place will take some time. You will soon learn that the Recluse may not always be withdrawn and quiet, you may also experience random outbursts and other forms of disrespect as she acts out of anger and mistrust. Be patient. Now there may not be a direct solution, you may have to make a call and do what is best for the child, you see there are various circumstances such as SA (sexual abuse), MA (mental abuse), and bullying, either way, stay engaged so that you can earn the students trust. The prescription is hope, and encouragement and helps the child find their voice.

"I have a question for you. In your wildest dreams…What would your life look like when you get older?"

I'm sure that the question may be met with, "I don't know," in the beginning but don't stop teaching the student to dream more. 'If you can see it, you can be it, never let anyone put you down or speak for you, your life is your own and you can be anything you like.'

Remember you may be the only one in their life who has encouraged them and it is a heavy responsibility that you will have to undertake, understanding that you have to power to help this child break away from their disparaging reality.

There is no such thing as favorites when you are teaching so that you do not single one child out from the gang, so try to keep this in mind. One technique will be "show and prove." To gain that trust you have to show the child that you are not like anyone else who may have hurt them, physically, mentally, and emotionally. Show and Prove works like has five pillars to it so make sure you practice it and use it often so that it becomes part of your arsenal.

Show and Prove

Step one, model reading in front of the classroom and have everyone in the class including the Recluse do the same. Anything that you do make sure that the whole class repeats.

Step two, celebrate the small things, any type of breakthrough you have with the Recluse, and incentivize it. Showing the student that it is noticed and appreciated. Coming from someone who is probably reminded every second of their life when they do things wrong, change the narrative.

Step three, encourage positive talk in the classroom. Whenever someone does something that shows signs of improvement or just a simple try, reward it with positive encouragement. Yes! Good Job! You can do it!

Step four is to set classroom goals, outside of just working on homework and class work, there should be a class-wide goal to keep each person involved. Now there may be times that the whole class does not finish the task as a whole but it builds character, and teamwork makes the dream work. Everyone takes accountability and wants each person to strive.

Step five, set a challenge and teach them that life is all about challenges; one step towards your challenge each day and being consistent will ultimately get them ready to work on completing tasks. Encourage them to never give up and give their best effort.

H.U.G.S.

This all comes from the H.U.G.S. method,

Help – help them break out of their shell

Unchain – free them from the fears and things that hold them back, it is said where the mind goes the body shall follow

Give – them hope, show them that all things are possible

Strength – building their self-esteem and using teamwork and group projects to uplift them where the classroom is a stronger unit that works together, they learn to depend on each other

The Copycat

We believe that teaching toward students' strengths has left the chat. Rarely do you find that approach outside of specialty schools in your public school system, has a one size fits approach. Now we have to ask ourselves: How do we fix this? In a perfect world, you would test for those abilities early on in the child's life then help with boosting the one area and follow up with all the other areas one at a time, teaching to their strengths. See if this makes any sense, maybe it will or not. Let's give it a try.

You know when a person loses one of their five senses; see, smell, taste, feel, and hear, a sense is heightened. Ok, now for years I could not smell or breathe out of my nose but I could enjoy the richness of food like nobody's business. I had a distinctive palate that could tell what was in any item. I missed my calling as a food taster. So, using that logic, what if the very thing that the child loves the most is boosted, cultivated, and supported? Could they naturally acclimate to learning the other subjects just the same?

Hmm, just a thought. Now correct me if I'm wrong or if am I on to something. If that doesn't quite get the point across, what about this: doing what you love? I will give you a scenario and mix in some future preparation. I like to say that one of our strong points is giving a person a roadmap of how to draw out a picture. So, let's talk about leading to discovery. Yes, finding out what that child loves and having a candid discussion on just how they will get there. Your goal is to help them find their strengths and weaknesses, then expound on them. Now there are going to be some other deterrents and speed bumps you will have to encounter but let's say considering them all here is the plan.

Praise What They Praise

Use the **Praise what they Praise method**, where you are not confrontational at all. The key to this method is to agree with them, then along the way review the key elements within their story. This will help you develop a keen ear for listening and comprehending, as to offer them an even better deal. Making sense of their logic is key and you will lose the battle if you are not equipped with an answer that puts their train of thought into a practical real-world scenario that fits. Outsmarting the fox.

"Hey Allan what do you want to be when you grow up?"

"I wanna be just like Jason!"

"Who is Jason?"

"Just the coolest guy I know, he has a lot of money, nice cars and all the women love him."

"What does Jason do for a living?"

"He gets money!"

Pause- This is a reality that most of us know all so well when dealing with underprivileged and underserved communities, unfortunately, certain statuses and ways of life are praised more than the person who went to school and became a doctor. The interaction is minimal to none, a very small percentage gives back or comes back to encourage a better way of

28

thinking and hope through mentorships in these communities. But I digress

"Ok, Jason... So, he has a good professional job, or owns his own business, that's nice he sounds like he has done well for himself and helps others in his community."

"No, he doesn't work, and yesterday he had to beat Man-man up for what he owed him. He handles his business. I wanna be just like him."

"Ohh wow, has he ever been arrested?"

"What!? Plenty of times and he keeps getting out! He beats the system they can't hold him!"

Pause-Teachers have their work cut out for them. In all seriousness, how can they teach a child like this who has other aspirations that have nothing to do with what they are trying to teach in the classroom? They are restricted to a curriculum that does not fit all situations. So knowingly, they are equipped to fail that student. They have no alternatives for Allan, it's not written in their teacher's handbook or from the nice Bachelor's or Master's Degree or teacher certifications and training. Not saying all are not equipped, but the curriculum they teach does not offer the real-life training they need to turn this child's perspective around.

Now Allan is failing in just about every subject. He is not accountable and wants to be the Class Clown, no one can reach him. He feels like his role model is being picked on when the teachers tell him he should want to be like someone else, not like him.

Let's try to reason with Allan to see if we can make some sense of the matter and open his eyes.

"Hey, Allan sounds like your friend Jason is living the life that he loves."

"Yeah, he aight, but now and then he complains about his baby momma stressing him and how he gotta watch out for the PoPo, it's just a way of life."

"I understand, so you want to be like Jason huh?"

"Yep, just like him."

"OK here's the deal, you know when you act up, I have to send you to the office or when you get a bad grade, I have to send notes home to your mom?"

"Yep, I hate that."

"Well, we gonna make a deal!"

"What's type of deal?"

"I am gonna make you a guarantee. I'm gonna make you better than Jason and you will have more things and not have to worry about what he goes through. Is that a deal?"

"Really? Wow, I didn't know teachers could do that type of stuff!"

"Yep, We can! So, let's get into it! Here is your assignment: Who do you want to be like when you grow up? List the 5 things about that person you like. Now list how you will be better than them."

"Here you go! I'm done!"

"Ok after reading over your assignment I regret to tell you that you will not be like Jason. Or even better than him."

"What! No way! I will be like him and better than him."

"Ok let me let you in on a little secret, that's if you want to listen."

"Ok, what is it?"

"Well, news flash, Jason knows how to read, write, spell, knows history, and is excellent in math."

"Huh?"

"Yes. He even is a pro in acting. Yep, he is the world's number one actor, a theater student."

"What do you mean he is an actor?"

"Yes, he acts like doing good in school is not cool, but in all reality, he is good at everything you are bad in."

"Man! I didn't know Jason was a nerd, ahh smart."

"Yes, how do you think he was able to do all those things, have the car money, and girls?"

"Because he's a thug!"

"Nope, wrong answer! He's good at acting and is well educated, well in a sense, he is literate."

"Literate?"

"Yes, He understands, comprehends, and executes his plans. You have to know some things to do all of those things."

"Man! I didn't know that!"

"So, for you to be better than Jason you will have to know more than him, take your education seriously, and not make the same mistakes that he has made and will make. You enjoy your freedom and the ability to make people laugh...right? So do yourself a favor, and be better than him in all ways."

"Wow, I didn't know all of that."

"My point exactly!!!"

The point I'm making is to have the student express what see as available to them, in their eyes. It is easily obtainable until they are given a glimpse of what it takes to get there. With more encouragement and giving them a different perspective, they will get where you are coming from. This tactic normally defuses the situation of the "them against us feeling," when they can compare their reality, which is a false sense of reality to what is real.

Another attribute of this program is filling in the gaps and giving them a head start in life. It suits them best to learn the important details in life now, mainly because these will be the things that they will have to understand and do for the rest of their lives. The following components that are necessary to operate efficiently and successfully are; Life skills, Communication skills, Interpersonal skills, the value of self-reflection, Accepting and giving criticism, Assertiveness, and self-esteem building, Stress management, Ethics and integrity, Business etiquette, and Finances. I know those may not be what you can teach them, but just as long as you can expose them to each subject in your own way, they will never forget the importance.

The Class Clown

For as long as you have been teaching, I'm sure you have run across the Class Clown, or if you are just starting to teach, brace yourself because the Class Clown is coming.

This child wants the limelight, and cannot stand being ignored, and finds everything funny except doing his or her work. They need the crowd's attention so much that they have become a nuisance and are keeping a lot of children distracted and not being able to do their work. The plan is to not just punish the Class Clown but to help cultivate their gifts.

I know, I know… what do you mean cultivate their gifts? If I pay attention to this one child and give them what they are asking for, then I will do a disservice to my other children who need me.

Calm down I do understand that's why I will be giving you some surefire ways to help deal with your Class Clown. With a lot of retraining, their attention, and compromise you will have one of your best students yet.

This child is one with an overactive mind, their imagination keeps them up at night bouncing all types of scenarios around in their heads. Nowadays you would categorize this child with ADD or ADHD and that would be a grave mistake. How this child processes the good and the bad in life is very different than others. I have seen some extremes where their home life can be just pure hell and you would never know it, to have a very enriching home life and they both need to exert their energies in various ways. You wonder just how can you deal with this type of child who will not shut up, they love to talk all day and cannot even help themselves even after being disciplined. We can start to implement the tactics and plans we put into play earlier on in the book to appeal to their logical side. Let's get into their space and also allow them to blow off some steam.

As a child, just like adults there is always a breaking point, we laugh to keep from crying. That phase of laughter is a coping mechanism and they want everyone to join in. This is one of the most challenging for children because there is a balance between what is your time management in the classroom and the participation of that child and the other students. It's a fine line, but when you master the art of communication things work themselves out.

You will need to get a better understanding of your student, the Class Clown.

If you have a Class Clown you have to follow these steps,

Put them to work.

Plain straightforward.

The Class Clown has misguided energy that you will have to put to good use.

The attention seeker wants to be the star of the show, you should let them be the star of the show, but not without compromise. Pull students to the side and remind them that the classroom is not set up for constant disruption, because that would not be fair to all of the students.

First, detention will give you some time to speak with the child and find out what their future goals are, normally speaking they will have a wild imagination so most of them have some clue about what they want to do, if not then you use that time to help them figure out what they should be in the future.

Most Class Clowns have great communication skills and a skillset of convincing people to listen to them and avoid listening to what's going on in the classroom. They lack respect because they do not value the job that the teacher has in front of them every day and the duties of the teacher. Now we have to reverse engineer this child's habits and give them a role in this featured film called The Classroom.

They love the spotlight and want to be the center of attention now they are going to be seen, your job as a teacher is to control your classroom and manage it well. Now with your new helper, things should run smoothly. Yes, in a perfect world that would be nice. This will be a tactic to gain control and take your class back or they will be forced to face heavy discipline. At least you have given them the options and a real-life lesson that you cannot get something for nothing.

Have them help with passing out papers, and checking around the classroom for things that are out of order. Remember, this gives them time to get out of their seats and roam for a certain amount of time. They feel like they have freedom, and in turn, you have a helper and things are getting done. Sounds like a fair trade to me.

One thing that I forgot to mention; when you do have that meeting with them, here is one question to ask, "What do you want to be when you get older?" The answer will determine exactly what items they need to work on now to be successful in their future endeavors.

With this process, we have found that it will either correct the bad behavior in the child or call their bluff. They will no longer want the attention or it will catapult them into enjoying the ways that they can be of service and not a nuisance in the classroom. Either way, it's a win for you.

In closing, we did not take a traditional approach to what a Class Clown is categorized as, so we touched on three other types that should not be left out, the Angry Child, the Recluse, and the Copycat. They all bring their own set of challenges to the classroom either disruptive outwardly or lacking class participation. As a teacher you have to deal with several problems and issues that are out of your scope, you have to do the best with what you have. We hope that this gives you a little more ammunition in the classroom to know that there's always a hidden factor behind how children behave in class.

Our overall purpose is to address these issues head-on and work the steps and tactics to overcome and help save a child's life, help improve their self-esteem, let them know that they are not alone, and get them the help and resources they need. Having one child in the classroom who is unruly will affect all of the students and rob them of their right to a decent education, it disrupts learning and takes valuable time away. Without techniques, the child will adhere to the process or refrain from the behavior. Wondering just where all of this is coming from, keeps teachers on their feet, and 99 percent of it comes from the home. Addressing the causes and dealing with the effects, may have you feeling hopeless, but we promise help is on the way.

Made in the USA
Columbia, SC
11 February 2024

31213854R00040